Chipeta
Ute Peacemaker

Chipeta
Ute Peacemaker

A NOW YOU KNOW BIO

Number Eleven in the Series

Cynthia S. Becker

Filter Press, LLC
Palmer Lake, Colorado

To the children of Colorado.
May you learn to love history
and the people who lived it.

ISBN: 978-0-86541-091-6
Library of Congress Control Number: 2008938507
Copyright © 2008 Cynthia S. Becker. All Rights Reserved.

Chipeta: Ute Peacemaker
Published by
Filter Press, LLC, P.O. Box 95, Palmer Lake, CO 80133
719-481-2420 • info@filterpressbooks.com

Printed in the United States of America

Contents

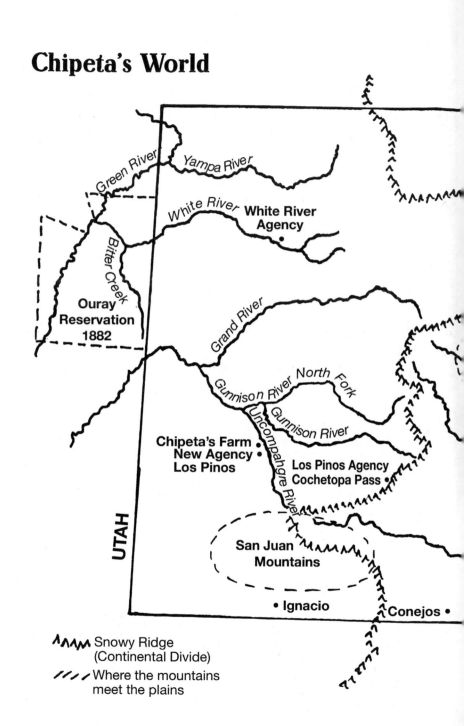

Chipeta's World

Green River

Yampa River

White River · White River Agency

Bitter Creek

Ouray Reservation 1882

Grand River

Gunnison River North Fork

Gunnison River

Uncompahgre River

Chipeta's Farm
New Agency ·
Los Pinos

Los Pinos Agency
Cochetopa Pass ·

UTAH

San Juan Mountains

· Ignacio

Conejos ·

ᴧᴧᴧᴧ Snowy Ridge
(Continental Divide)

//// Where the mountains
meet the plains

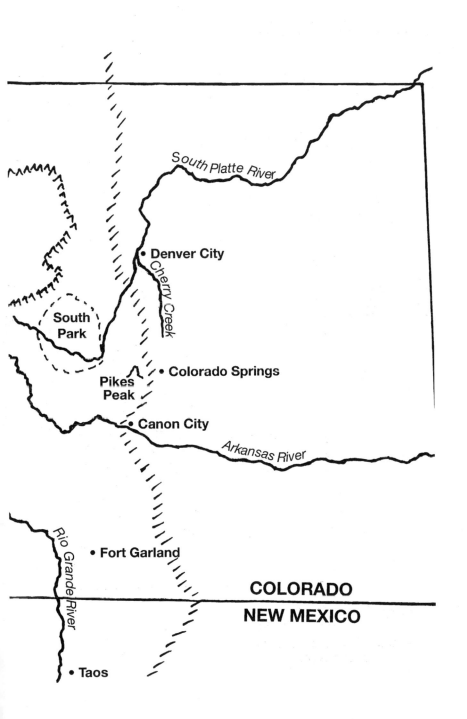

Chipeta…showed character through extremely turbulent times in our country's history. Our nation's leaders in Washington, D.C. sought out her ideas for peace. She demonstrated the…six pillars of character…caring, fairness, respect, responsibility, trustworthiness, and citizenship.

From the Chipeta Elementary School web site
Colorado Springs, Colorado

Prologue

"Gold!" The prospector's shouts echoed through the valleys north of Pikes Peak. The wind carried that word among the Noochee, "the people," who lived in the Rocky Mountains. Chipeta, a Ute Indian girl of fifteen winters, had no idea how that word would shape her future.

"Gold!" That word slithered down streambeds and spread like wildfire across open prairie. It tickled the ears of men in the East, daring them to cross the wide plains and seek their fortunes.

The New York Times
September 20, 1858
"The Gold Excitement in Kansas"
From the Leavenworth Times, 10th inst.

Leavenworth was agog yesterday. There was a buzz of excitement throughout the entire day. "Gold" was upon the lips of all, and the "Pike's Peak" acquired an immense deal of notoriety...

Mr. Elmore King gave us a brief account of his experience in the gold region. He went out in the

Spring and left on the 27th of last July. During this time he was engaged in prospecting, and never failed to discover the "pure ore." Several companies were regularly engaged in the work of digging, and, as a general thing, took out from five to ten dollars a day per man.

All they had was common pans, and even these were scarce. A man, with proper tools for obtaining gold, could secure from ten to fifty dollars a day.

Men left jobs, homes, and families. They hurried west in wagons, on horseback, and by foot. Within a year, 50,000 men, and a few women, panned the streams and dug into the rocky ground hunting for gold.

Merchants followed the gold seekers. They turned ancient Ute pathways into roads. Their wagons hauled food, clothing and tools to mining camps. Boarding houses, stores, and saloons expanded the camps. Miners built houses and sent for their families. Doctors and dentists, school teachers and seamstresses, blacksmiths and cooks all found work in the camps. Towns sprang up along the eastern foothills. Montana City, St. Charles, Auraria, and Denver City became supply stations for the mining camps.

At first, the Utes welcomed these newcomers. The white men were eager to trade flour, sugar, and tobacco for warm buffalo robes. The Utes saw problems as the number of miners and settlers increased. The newcomers cut all the trees from hillsides to build cabins and towns. They dumped mining scrap and rubbish in the streams. They hunted the deer, elk, and buffalo the Utes needed for survival.

The Utes tried to scare away the newcomers by stealing their horses and supplies. When that didn't work, the Utes threatened, and sometimes killed, men, women, and children. Driven by gold fever, the newcomers were not about to give up. They intended to stay, and they outnumbered the Utes.

A white man who filed a claim and paid a fee received a title on paper. He owned a piece of land and its contents. The Utes did not understand such "titles." Every Ute child knew the Shining Mountains had always belonged to their people. They understood their **territory**, just as they knew which areas of the Plains belonged to the Cheyenne, the Kiowa, and the Arapaho Indians.

"Gold!" The word sparked a long battle over land and changed the Ute way of life forever.

CHIPETTA.

Chipeta was photographed during her trip to Washington, D.C., by Matthew Brady. She is wearing traditional buckskin with fringe and a wide sash, and beaded jewelry. The photo is dated January 29, 1880.

1 A Ute Childhood

Chipeta was born in the Rocky Mountains of North America in 1843. She had an older brother named Sapovanara and a younger brother called McCook. Chipeta was seven years old when McCook was born and she loved taking care of the boy. He was never far from her side for the rest of her life.

Chipeta's family was part of the **Tabeguache** (tab-uh-wash) band of Ute Indians. Six bands occupied the Shining Mountains. The Tabeguache claimed the valleys of the Gunnison and **Uncompahgre** Rivers and the surrounding area.

Ute families did not live in one place. They roamed a large territory and moved with the changing seasons. In winter, many families camped together in a protected valley. Winter was great storytelling time. The family gathered around the fire at night and Chipeta's father or grandfather told stories about the Ute people. They told the same stories over and over. Stories recorded the history of people with no written language.

Chipeta's family included her mother's parents and her mother's sisters. A man joined his new wife's family when he married. Chipeta's mother owned the teepee and all the household utensils. Chipeta's father measured his wealth in horses. He hunted meat and protected the camp from enemies.

Ute girls learned women's duties at a young age. Chipeta helped her mother clean and preserve animal skins for clothing. Furry buffalo hides became warm blankets. Chipeta's mother taught her to make dresses, shirts, leggings, and moccasins. When she received her first sewing **awl**, Chipeta made a small leather bag to hold this important tool. It hung from her wide belt so she would not lose it. Adding designs to clothing with colored beads was Chipeta's favorite part of sewing. She was known for her skill at beading and continued to make beaded items into her old age.

After the long winter, families gathered for the Bear Dance. They feasted and danced for several days to wake the bear from his winter sleep and welcome spring. Then, families went their separate ways to gather summer foods.

The valleys were green with new plants and the streams were full of fish. Sometimes Chipeta's father caught a beaver and they made a special feast of the tail. They moved up the mountain sides as the fruits and berries ripened. They ate the first picking of fruits and dried the rest for winter. Chipeta learned where to find plants to eat and to use for medicine.

The family kept moving eastward. In autumn, they joined other families for the buffalo hunt in South Park. When she was little, Chipeta stayed with elders and other children during the hunt. By age ten, she helped her mother cut the meat into strips and hang it over sticks to dry. The dried buffalo meat was their main winter food. As the air turned cold, Chipeta's family returned to a mountain valley for winter camp.

The Utes treated the land with great respect. During the time between winters, they walked and rode long distances, singing songs to maintain peace with nature. They left gifts to assure the land they traveled would welcome them next season.

Chipeta's family had limited experience with the world outside the Shining Mountains. By the time Chipeta was born, trappers and traders came into the mountains. Chipeta's family welcomed these visitors, but did not allow them to build homes or stay in Ute territory. The Utes traded buffalo robes and ponies for tobacco, guns, bullets, knives, and beads.

Chipeta was eight years old when she first saw her future husband, Ouray (oo-ray). He came to the winter camp with his brother, sister, and father. The family came from Taos where Pueblo Indians and Spanish people lived. Ouray's father was a Ute man. His mother's people were Jicarilla Apache (hih-kuh-ree-uh ah-pa-chee) Indians. After Ouray's mother died, his father returned to his Ute family. Ouray and his brother, Quenche (kin-shay), were handsome young men. Chipeta was more interested in their sister, Tsashin (sah-shin), who was near her own age and a potential playmate.

Eighteen-year-old Ouray was a most unusual young man. He spoke four languages — Spanish, Ute, Apache, and English. As boys, Ouray and Quenche lived with a Spanish rancher's family. The boys herded sheep, and their father received their pay. The rancher

Yulé et Quincy, chefs des Yutes (bande des Sahquatches). — Dessin de Janet Lange d'après une photographie.

As young men, Ouray and his brother Quenche were pictured in the French magazine, Le Tour du Monde, Vol. 17, 1868.

was good to the boys, but life was very different from the Indian camp. They lived in a house instead of a teepee. They wore clothes made of woven fabric instead of animal hides. They learned to speak Spanish so well that Ouray said he thought in Spanish.

The United States Army arrived at Taos in 1846 with many men and guns. Ouray learned a little English from the soldiers. He observed the soldiers' ways and use of guns and cannons during the Mexican-American War. The number of men and powerful weapons made a lasting impression on him.

When Ouray joined his Ute family in 1851, he knew more about the world outside their mountain homeland than any other Ute. He set out to prove to his new relatives that he was a skilled hunter and a powerful warrior.

Know More!

Ute Names

Spelling of Ute names was usually based on how the names sounded to English speaking people. Ouray, for example, is found in documents as Ulé, Ulay, Ula, Uré, and Uray — the Arrow. Names used in this book may be found spelled differently in other sources.

Ouray married a woman named Black Mare, and they had a son. They called the boy Pahlone. Black Mare died when Pahlone was a small child. Some stories say she was bitten by a rattlesnake. Other stories say she died in childbirth. Ouray later said she died along with a girl child.

When a Ute woman died, one of her sisters or cousins took over care of the household and the children. The family chose Chipeta to care for Pahlone. She loved the little boy, and Ouray was pleased by the way Chipeta managed Pahlone and the teepee. Before long Ouray, Chipeta, and Pahlone became a family. Chipeta's little brother, McCook, spent so much time with them that Ouray treated him like a second son.

2 Wife and Mother

Chipeta was content with her new life as wife and mother. Ouray wanted to become a Ute chief. He built a circle of loyal young Tabeguache men who considered him their leader.

Ouray did not forget friends from his youth in Taos. One friend, a white man named Kit Carson, opened an unusual path to power for Ouray. Carson spoke both Spanish and Ute. He was the Indian **agent** for the Jicarilla Apaches and the Muache (moo-ah-chee) Ute band, who made a peace treaty with the United States government in 1848.

As Chipeta and Ouray began their life together, miners found gold on the east side of the mountains. The search for gold led the miners farther into Ute territory. Kit Carson told Ouray the miners would not leave without a fight, and there were more miners than Utes. Carson explained the white man's method of owning land. He said the Utes needed a title to their land, written on paper so the white men would understand. Carson suggested a treaty with the United States government as a way get this title.

In October 1859, Ouray took some chiefs to Taos for a talk with Carson about problems with the miners. Carson wrote in his annual report that year, "...the hunting grounds of the Tabeguache being in the section of the country where the whites are in search of gold, their game is becoming scarce; much of it being killed by the settlers..."

Lafayette Head became Indian agent for the Utes in 1861. He used his ranch near **Conejos** as his office. Head spoke English and Spanish, but not the Ute language. Kit Carson recommended Ouray as a skilled interpreter. Agent Head hired him at a salary of $500 per year. Suddenly, Chipeta and Ouray had something very unusual, white man's money to spend.

When miners and settlers organized Colorado **Territory** in 1861, Kit Carson urged Ouray to get a treaty. Ouray and Agent Head rode to Denver City to meet Territorial Governor John Evans. The governor wrote a letter to president of the United States proposing a treaty council with the Utes.

Chipeta and Ouray joined a buffalo hunt on the plains north of Denver City in the fall of 1861. The miners and settlers had killed off most of the South Park herd. During the hunt, Arapaho Indians raided the camp and rode off with Tsashin. Ouray and his father led the chase, but the kidnappers escaped with the girl. Seeing how quickly a child could be stolen, Chipeta kept Pahlone close by her side.

Late in 1862, Ouray left on a long trip. Governor Evans made arrangements for Ouray to cross the wide plains to council with the head chief of the United States. No Ute had ever been so far away. Agent Head and six of Ouray's men, including Quenche, went along.

Such a trip was dangerous. Chipeta feared something would happen to Ouray, but she was also proud of him. She made him a fine new buckskin shirt with matching leggings decorated with beadwork.

The Ute **delegation** left Conejos on the first day of February 1863. Chipeta and Pahlone stayed in winter camp, and McCook took over Ouray's chores. Agent Head delivered a flock of sheep to feed the families while the men were away.

Ouray did not return until June. He had stories of many adventures to entertain Chipeta, Pahlone, and McCook. The delegation traveled thirty sleeps by wagon to a town called St. Joe. Then they rode a train, a covered wagon without horses that rolled along spitting fire and smoke. The train traveled far north past great lakes larger than any Ouray had ever seen. Agent Head said the north route was long but safe. The white men were fighting a war among themselves in the middle and southern part of the country.

Washington City was a strange and noisy place. It was much larger than Denver City. Some buildings were so large the entire Ute band could set up camp

Know More!

Lafayette Head

Lafayette Head (1825-1897) settled in New Mexico Territory in 1849 after serving in the U.S. Army during the Mexican-American War. He developed a large sheep ranch in the San Luis Valley. In 1854, he was a founder of Conejos, one of the first permanent settlements in Colorado. He was elected to the territorial legislature in 1874 and the constitutional convention in 1875. Head wrote sections of the state constitution about agriculture and irrigation. He served as the first Lieutenant Governor of the State of Colorado from 1877-1879.

inside. At night, little fires burned on top of poles lining the roads to scare away the dark.

The Utes talked with many chiefs in Washington City. Ouray stretched his arm high in the air as he described the head chief of the United States, the tall, thin Abraham Lincoln. Ouray showed everyone the shiny black stick with the silver tip that Lincoln gave him as a token of friendship. After their talk, Lincoln agreed to send government men to the mountains for a council after the autumn buffalo hunt.

Ouray and his men spent the summer visiting the scattered Ute camps. They invited every chief and head man to the important October council with President Lincoln's men.

The summer of 1863 brought a great surprise. Tsashin came home. Chipeta listened to the girl's frightening tale of two years as an Arapaho captive. U.S. Army soldiers rescued Tsashin, and one of the men took her home to his wife. The couple wanted her to live

Know More!

The capital of the United States was called Washington City until 1871. By act of Congress the city was joined with the surrounding District of Columbia.

with them. They were kind, Tsashin said, but she missed her own family. She left while the couple was away visiting friends. She walked many days until she happened into a Northern Ute camp. They brought her to Ouray's camp. The reunion with Tsashin was happy but brief. A Northern Ute medicine man asked Tsashin to marry him and live with his people. She accepted his offer.

Denver Public Library, Western History Collection, X-19251

Chipeta and Ouray were married for twenty-one years, 1859-1880. Unlike most Ute wives, Chipeta often accompanied Ouray on his travels. This photograph was made in Denver in 1872 or 1873.

3 Tragedy

Many Ute families gathered for the annual buffalo hunt in September 1863. They traveled onto the plains north of Denver City to find a herd. Ouray took six-year-old Pahlone along to a hunters' camp near the herd. Chipeta stayed in the main camp where the women waited to cut and dry the buffalo meat and clean the hides.

One night, a group of Plains Indians raided the hunters' camp. Ouray and his men fought the attackers. When the battle was over, Pahlone was missing. The men searched for him, but the attackers and Pahlone had disappeared. In spite of her pain, Chipeta worked with the other women taking down the teepees and loading the buffalo meat on pack horses. The Utes retreated into the mountains.

Losing Pahlone stunned Ouray and Chipeta. The teepee felt empty without their lively boy. Ouray asked Agent Head to contact other Indian agents, trappers, traders, and anyone else who could find Pahlone. Chipeta kept busy with very physical work that followed a buffalo hunt. She cleaned and **tanned** the heavy animal hides. Ouray focused on the coming council meeting.

The great council met at Agent Head's home. Fifteen hundred Tabeguache Utes, three chiefs of the Capote Ute band, and one Muache chief arrived for opening day on October 1, 1863. Chipeta set up her teepee in the large camp that spread across the pasture. She helped new arrivals with their teepees and visited among the women. Sometimes they spoke of their husbands' feelings about a treaty.

President Lincoln's personal assistant led the government team. A small group of soldiers, commanded by Colonel John Chivington, arrived with the government men. During opening ceremonies, the soldiers demonstrated a powerful cannon that knocked down a stand of trees with one shot.

Ouray and Agent Head worked as a team, just as they had done during the council in Washington City.

Ouray interpreted from Ute to Spanish. Agent Head turned Spanish to English for the government men. Ouray was a commanding presence. The government men saw him as the Ute leader. On the seventh day, the Utes had a treaty.

The Tabeguache gave up use of their lands east of the Snowy Ridge, as people in Washington City called the **Continental Divide**. They gained title to all their territory west of the ridge. The government called the Ute land a **reservation**. In exchange for land, the Tabeguache Utes received **annuities**. The government promised to deliver $20,000 worth of food and household goods every year for ten years. The government also promised 5 American stallions, 750 cattle, and

Know More!

Colonel John Chivington

Little more than a year after he accompanied President Lincoln's men to the council at Conejos, Colonel Chivington led the Sand Creek Massacre. On November 29, 1864, Chivington's troops attacked a peaceful village of 100 Cheyenne lodges camped along Sand Creek. Chief Black Kettle had given up fighting and believed his people were under government protection. Chivington's men killed more than 150 Indians that day, then looted and burned the camp.

3,500 sheep. So long as the Utes kept their part of the agreement, the United States government pledged to protect Ute territory.

The chiefs and the government men smoked a peace pipe. Nine Ute chiefs, including Ouray and Quenche, signed the treaty with "X" marks. Seven Ute leaders who were "most cooperative" received silver medals. Ouray wore his Lincoln Peace Medal for photographs taken later in Denver City.

Chipeta's life did not return to normal after the treaty council. Pahlone was still missing. The treaty took away some of her favorite campgrounds, places she had known since childhood. Adding to her problems, Governor Evans had plans for her husband. The governor asked Ouray to settle disputes between Utes and white settlers. Ouray traveled great distances to do what the governor asked.

Chipeta was lonely without Ouray and Pahlone. She decided to do something unusual. She asked to travel with Ouray. He was happy to have her company. Chipeta watched and listened as settlers and Utes stated their complaints. Ouray asked questions and compared statements before making his decision. If he found a Ute had stolen a horse, Ouray told the Ute to

Colorado Historical Society, #10038924.

Ouray is shown in 1870 wearing the Lincoln Peace Medal and holding a silver tipped cane, given to him by Abraham Lincoln.

"Ouray was a good man, a man who would have measured up to a high standard in any civilized community...The Indians respected him and also feared him...To disobey his orders meant severe punishment and often death...he still was most particular in establishing the truth of a charge before proceeding with punishment."
— Major James Thompson, Special Agent to the Utes 1869-1874

return it. Ouray's own men made sure the Utes followed his orders. If Ouray believed a Ute was not at fault, he said so. He gained a reputation among the white settlers as a fair man. That made him even more popular with the governor.

As the couple traveled to Ute camps, Chipeta visited with the women. She learned from the women how their men felt about problems facing the Utes. This information-gathering role became important as her husband rose in power. Some Utes came to hate Ouray. Chipeta was welcomed in camps where Ouray dared not set his foot. Ouray learned to trust the information Chipeta supplied, and her advice.

Josefa Carson was Chipeta's first non-Indian female friend. In 1866, Ouray's old friend, Kit Carson,

Know More!

Presidential Peace Medals

Peace medals looked like large silver coins. Indian chiefs received the medals as symbols of friendship with the U.S. government. Lewis and Clark gave Jefferson Medals to Indian chiefs during their western exploration. Indian chiefs often received medals when they settled a treaty with the government. Benjamin Harrison (1878-1881) was the last president to give peace medals. By his time, most Indians had accepted treaties and lived on reservations.

Maria Josefa Jaramillo (1828-1868) was 15 when she married 33-year-old
Kit Carson. Josefa came from a prominent New Mexico family and was a
sister-in-law of William Bent, governor of New Mexico Territory.
She died in 1868 after the birth of her seventh child. Kit Carson died
less than a month later.

commanded Fort Garland. Ouray and Chipeta arrived in late summer with 100 lodges of Tabeguache Utes. Josefa managed a household of six children. She set her table with china and silver and invited Chipeta and Ouray to eat with the family. Kit Carson enjoyed his active youngsters. Watching this happy family renewed Chipeta's and Ouray's interest in children. Soon after visiting the Carsons, they began to adopt abandoned children.

Some Capote Utes came to Fort Garland to council with Carson and Ouray. One evening, the Carsons hosted a supper for the visitors. Chipeta and Ouray were included. A Capote man became angry and hit one of the Carson daughters with his riding whip. Kit Carson attacked the man. Josefa stepped into the fight, grabbed her husband's arm, and commanded him to stop. She talked to Kit until he was calm. Her action prevented a much larger fight that night. Chipeta did not forget Josefa's brave example.

4 Government Housing

C hipeta stayed in camp while Ouray led another delegation to Washington City in 1868. He settled a new treaty. Among other things, the treaty gave the Tabeguache their own agent. **Los Pinos** Agency was built near the top of **Cochetopa** (coe chuh toe pah) Pass in 1869. Log buildings housed blacksmith and carpenter shops, a mill, a store, a school room, and quarters for agency employees. The barn and corrals sat a short distance away. The agent's three room house served as his office. Ouray continued his job as interpreter for the new agency. To Chipeta's surprise, the agency included a small two-room **adobe** house for the interpreter. Chipeta preferred her teepee.

A merchant named Otto Mears was appointed agency trader, to buy and deliver supplies for Los Pinos.

Mears hired Ouray to hunt meat for the agency staff. With a government house and two paychecks, Ouray and Chipeta did not need government annuities. Many Utes wondered how Ouray got such a good deal.

Settlers moved into what had been Ute land. Chipeta showed new arrivals the safe place to cross rivers swollen with spring snow melt. She offered food to people who were unprepared for the hard winters. She made friends among the settlers. Chipeta and Ouray returned to visit in summers. They raised their teepee in favorite old campsites that had become someone's ranch.

Chipeta found a new female friend in May 1872. Charles Adams became the fourth Ute agent in three years at Los Pinos. His wife, Margaret, served as teacher for the agency school. Although Chipeta encouraged families to bring children to school, few came. Margaret was often the only woman living at the agency. She welcomed times when Chipeta was there. The two women and their husbands often ate dinner together in the agent's house.

Before the ink was dry on the 1868 treaty, miners were illegally exploring Ute land on the west side of the mountains. In the reservation's San Juan Mountains,

While at Los Pinos Indian Agency, August 19, 1874, the famous photographer of the early West, William Henry Jackson, photographed Chipeta. Chipeta's clothes were often decorated with her own beadwork. Here she wears Navajo silver jewelry as well.

the miners found rich deposits of silver and gold. The miners thought it was unfair that they could not have the minerals which the Utes did not want. The miners pressured the government to reclaim the San Juans.

The new territorial governor, Edward McCook, supported the miners. He had no use for the Indians. The governor asked President Ulysses S. Grant to open new treaty talks. He told the president the best solution would be to move all Utes out of Colorado. President Grant agreed to negotiate with the Utes. In the meantime, Grant ordered federal troops to guard the reservation against miners.

Through her contacts with Ute women, Chipeta heard rumors making the rounds of Ute camps. The people feared Ouray would give up the San Juans. Chipeta told her husband how the people felt. Many Utes believed Ouray had gained his house and government salary by trading away Ute land. They did not trust him to protect their remaining land. The rumors grew and several men tried to kill Ouray. One of those men was Chipeta's brother, Sapovanara.

Five men hid inside the Los Pinos blacksmith shop that Ouray visited every morning. The blacksmith, George Hardman, saw the men and warned Ouray before he entered the shop. Sapovanara attacked with an ax, but powerful Ouray pinned him to the ground. The other four men slipped from their hiding places and ran out the back door.

Chipeta arrived as Ouray reached for his knife to kill Sapovanara. Both men froze at her command. She took Ouray's knife from his belt and talked until both men were calm. Then, Chipeta negotiated a truce between her husband and her brother. After that day, Sapovanara proved his loyalty so well that he became Ouray's second-in-command.

Ouray made another trip to Washington in December 1872. The government offered to buy the San Juans. Ouray refused.

In June 1873, Agent Adams took Ouray on a secret trip. Ouray returned to give Chipeta surprising news. He met with Felix Brunot, **Commissioner** of Indian Affairs. Brunot offered to bring Pahlone home, but Ouray must sell the San Juans. Brunot asked to come to Los Pinos for a council with the chiefs. He said he would bring Pahlone.

Eighteen hundred Utes camped in the meadow near Los Pinos for the August 15, 1873 council. Chipeta waited on the agent's front porch to see her grown up boy. Brunot arrived alone. He said Pahlone refused to come. The boy lived with the Arapaho and had a new name, Friday. The council met. Ouray refused Brunot's new offer to buy the San Juans.

In October, Brunot called Ouray and the men of the 1872 delegation back to Washington. Chipeta waited in winter camp near the junction of the Gunnison and Uncompahgre Rivers. Ouray returned in November. His report of the trip shocked Chipeta. President Grant made a new offer to buy the San Juans. This time the chiefs agreed to sell. After the deal was made, Ouray met the boy called Friday.

Ouray described the scene for Chipeta. On November 3, 1873, he and the Ute chiefs entered a room filled with government men and delegations of Arapaho and Cheyenne chiefs. The government wanted Ouray, Powder Face of the Arapaho, and Stone Calf of the Cheyenne to make peace. The three chiefs shook hands to satisfy the government men.

Brunot introduced the man known as Friday. The young man looked Ouray in the eye and said, "I am an Arapaho. The Utes are my enemies."

"This is not my son," Ouray told all the men in the room.

Ouray did not hear what the government men said in private after the meeting. They all thought Friday looked enough like Ouray to be his son. Friday died not long after meeting Ouray.

That winter Chipeta and Ouray welcomed a group of twenty-nine miners who wandered into camp. The men came from the west on their way to the gold fields in the San Juans. Ouray suggested they stay in the Ute camp until spring. He said the winter snows in the high mountains made travel dangerous. Many of the miners stayed.

One group of six miners started out in early February for Los Pinos. Chipeta gave the men ten days worth of food for the seventy-mile trip. When Chipeta and Ouray returned to Los Pinos in the summer, they learned that only one of the miners survived the trip. Alferd Packer told the agency staff his companions died from cold and hunger. When the bodies were found, some had bullet wounds. Packer later admitted he survived by eating some of his companions. He was convicted of murder and sent to prison.

In the late summer of 1874, the men of the Hayden Survey visited Los Pinos. They were assigned by the government to map and photograph western lands. William Henry Jackson was the official photographer. He visited Ouray and Chipeta and described their little house in his diary:

> Room was very simply, even rudely furnished, couches of rough boards forming the beds, a few chairs & stools, [a] beaded dress and a few prints from illustrated papers decorated the walls.

Jackson set up a studio on the agent's front porch. Ouray agreed to let Jackson take his picture, but Chipeta was afraid of the camera. Rumor among the Utes claimed the camera stole a person's spirit. Ouray worked hard to convince her to sit for a photo. Jackson

Know More!

William Henry Jackson and the Hayden Survey
William Henry Jackson (1843-1942) was a photographer and artist. From 1870-1878 he served as official photographer for the Hayden Geological and Geographic Survey of the Territories. Through Jackson's photos, people in the eastern United States saw the rugged beauty of America's West for the first time. His images of Yellowstone helped make that area the first national park. Jackson later settled in Denver and opened a photo studio.

commented in his diary that he could see Ouray was very proud of Chipeta:

> When she finally sat before the camera, she smiled like...[a] bride...The doeskin of which her dress was made was almost as white as cotton, and nearly as soft as silk. From every edge and seam hung thick white fringes, twelve or fifteen inches long, while a pretty trimming of bead work and porcupine-quill embroidery set off the costume.

In September, Felix Brunot returned to Los Pinos to complete sale of the San Juans. The chiefs signed the final agreement, which none of them could read. Brunot did not tell the chiefs he had added something to the document they signed. The treaty named Ouray Head Chief of all the Utes and doubled his annual salary to $1,000.

The treaty moved the Los Pinos agency to the Uncompahgre Valley. In the spring of 1875, Ouray and a new agent chose the site. Nine miles north of the agency, Ouray selected a 160 acre tract where he and Chipeta would live. The government wanted the Utes to settle down and become farmers. Ouray and Chipeta decided to be role models.

With his new salary, Ouray hired workers to build a house, barns, and corrals. By late summer, he and Chipeta moved to their big new home. The agent's wife helped Chipeta buy furnishings. Ouray hired a woman to cook and keep the house and men to do the farm work.

Know More!

The Tabeguache Utes

The Tabeguache Utes became known as the Uncompahgre Utes after their agency moved to the valley of that name in 1875. The name remains Tabeguache in this book to avoid confusion.

5 Trouble in the North

Chipeta found life in the Uncompahgre Valley peaceful. Ouray no longer traveled long distances to settle disputes. He stayed close to the farm. Chiefs, and the agent, came to the house to council with Ouray around a sturdy table built by the agency carpenter. Friends and relatives came to visit. Many preferred to pitch their tents in the pasture rather than sleep in the house.

While Ouray stayed at home, Chipeta enjoyed the annual Bear Dance, held in a grove of **piñon** trees north of the agency. She rode out in the valley to visit friends and made longer trips to visit Tsashin and other relatives. Chipeta always returned from visits with news for Ouray.

When he felt well, Ouray took short hunting trips. Often, Chipeta went along. She enjoyed the brief return to the life without a house, and she was a crack shot with a rifle. Sometimes the couple rode to a mineral hot springs where Ouray soaked his aches and pains. A Mexican worker taught Chipeta to play the guitar. She learned a few Spanish songs Ouray knew from childhood. Her mellow voice soothed her husband's bad days.

Two problems clouded life on the new farm— Ouray's health and complaints from the Northern Utes at the White River Agency.

Ouray suffered headaches, back pains, and fatigue. In the summer of 1876, McCook traveled with Ouray and Chipeta to see Dr. Lewis in Cañon City. He diagnosed a kidney ailment called Bright's Disease.

Runners brought news from the other Ute bands. The news from White River Utes was always about their new agent, Nathan Meeker. He did not understand the Ute way of life. Meeker was a newspaper man before he became the Indian agent. He thought it would be simple to teach the Utes to be farmers, but everything he did made them mad.

Denver Public Library, Western History Collection, X-30595.

Chipeta and Ouray lived in this house in the Uncompaghre Valley near Montrose, Colorado, from 1875 to 1881. She received $5000 for the 160-acre farm when the Utes were forced to move to Utah.

When the Utes did not act as Meeker wanted, he threatened them with punishment. Ute men counted their wealth in horses. Racing one man's horse against another was a favorite sport. Meeker plowed up the racing field. Nicaagut, a White River chief known to white men as Jack, came to see Ouray. Nicaagut wanted help in getting a new agent. Ouray asked the Tabeguache agent to write to Washington about the problem.

On a visit to Tsashin, Chipeta noticed that the Utes bought food and supplies from a store on Bear River.

She asked why they did not get rations from the agency. Chipeta learned that Agent Meeker punished what he called bad Utes by not giving them food rations.

In September 1878, a few White River Utes stole horses from nearby ranchers and shot a white man. Newspapers suggested the beginning of a Ute war. Troubles continued. In July 1879, Governor Pitkin reported to the Commissioner of Indian Affairs the White River Utes were off the reservation and burning millions of acres of forest. He requested military help to control them. On August 20, 1879, a group of White

Know More!

How the incidents at Meeker began

Nathan Meeker threatened to bring soldiers to the reservation. They would take disagreeable Utes to prison, Meeker said. One day, Ute scouts saw a line of Army troops marching toward the reservation. They remembered Meeker's threat. Nicaagut rode down to talk with the troop commander. Nicaagut asked the commander and one or two soldiers to come with him to the agency for a talk with Agent Meeker. The commander refused. Nicaagut and his men set up an ambush. When other Utes heard about the fight with soldiers, they killed Meeker and the agency men. They caught the women trying to escape with the children.

River chiefs met with the governor in Denver. The chiefs explained the problems with Agent Meeker. The chiefs said they wanted to avoid more trouble. They asked for a new agent. The governor did nothing.

Chipeta opened her door to worse news on October 1, 1879. A runner reported White River Utes were in the midst of a battle with U.S. Army soldiers. A number of soldiers were dead. The White River Utes wanted help.

Chipeta sent a farm worker to bring Ouray back from hunting. She sent other workers to bring the Tabeguache chiefs to the farm for a council. Chipeta listened as Ouray and the chiefs talked. They worried that their young men would ride off to help the White River Utes. These young men grew up hearing stories of great battles in the past. They were anxious to prove their own skills at war. Ouray understood how the young men felt. He talked about going to White River. He said he might like to join one last great fight. Chipeta talked him out of that idea. Charles Adams later described Chipeta's influence on Ouray:

> Ouray told me afterwards that during that night
> he suffered more agony of mind than ever before

in his life; that something seemed to call him north to the home of his White River brothers, if only to stop the fighting, but that Chipeta wept and begged all night…Her gentle counsel prevailed and by morning Ouray had decided to order Douglas [a White River chief] to retreat…

Before Ouray could send his order, another runner arrived from White River. Agent Meeker and all the agency workers were dead. The Utes held Meeker's wife and daughter, plus another white woman and her two children, as **hostages**.

Word of the situation at White River spread across the state by telegraph, newspaper, and rumor. Governor Pitkin put 1,000 men on alert to defend white citizens. John C. Bell of the Pitkin Guards recalled the governor's order: "…consider all Indians off the reservation hostile, and bring them in, dead or alive, and we will determine their [attitude] afterward."

Rumors grew. *Two thousand Utes on the warpath… Whole towns wiped out by Indian attacks.* Citizens gathered weapons and prepared to defend themselves. The governor called for troops from Kansas, Texas, and New Mexico. Colorado was on the edge of war.

Meanwhile, the Utes huddled on their reservations, fearing what might happen next. Chipeta's house was a beehive of activity. Runners came and went. Chiefs waited for news. They held councils day and night. It was hunting season and many Utes roamed off the reservation to old familiar hunting places. Ouray sent runners to bring every Ute hunter home. He feared they would be shot by any white citizen who saw them.

Two weeks passed. The Meeker women were still hostages. U.S. **Secretary of the Interior** Carl Schurz asked Charles Adams to help. Adams was no longer an Indian agent, but he was the only man trusted by everyone involved.

Chipeta greeted Charles Adams at her door on October 18, 1879. Adams was shocked to see how old and tired both Chipeta and Ouray appeared. The three friends talked into the night and came up with a plan. Ouray sent a messenger to tell the White River chiefs: "Adams is coming to get the hostages." Adams rode out with a trusted group of Tabeguache men led by Sapovanara. At White River, Adams convinced the Army to leave the reservation. The White River chiefs released the hostages.

The Meeker women and children arrived at Chipeta's home on October 29. Meeker's daughter, Josephine, said Chipeta cried as she welcomed them.

> Chipeta...did everything possible to make us comfortable. We found carpets on the floor and curtains on the windows, lamps on the tables and stoves in the rooms, with fires burning. We were given a whole house, and after supper we went to bed without much fear.

The "Meeker Massacre" was national news. The *New York Times* carried front page reports for thirty days. Colorado newspapers carried anti-Ute headlines such as, "The Utes Must Go." Colorado citizens were angry. The deaths at White River were the last straw. The citizens wanted the Utes moved out of the state.

Ouray, Charles Adams, and one other man were appointed by Secretary Schurz to make a formal investigation of the Meeker incident. They began work in November. The Meeker women named ten Utes who killed the white men and took the hostages. Ouray asked to move the investigation to

Washington, D.C. He argued that no Ute could get a fair hearing in Colorado. Secretary Schurz agreed and quickly made arrangements. Charles Adams recommended Chipeta as a member of the new delegation to Washington.

6 Washington Adventure

When Chipeta and the Ute men boarded the Denver and Rio Grande train in Alamosa, crowds yelled hateful words. Soldiers held off angry citizens. They changed trains in Pueblo where a mob of 2,000 people threw rocks and shouted "Hang the red devils!" As the train rolled eastward, people in small towns lined the tracks. They shook their fists as the Utes passed by. Another mob waited in Chicago.

Chipeta was relieved to find the Baltimore and Potomac Station empty when they arrived in Washington, D.C. It was early Sunday morning, January 11, 1880. One reporter for the *Washington Post* met the train. His description of Chipeta appeared in the Monday morning newspaper:

She is a large squatty woman, about forty-five years old with broad flat features, a large round head and long black hair parted in the center and thrown carelessly at either side, almost conceal-ing her features. Her form was enveloped in the folds of a large black and gray woolen shawl... the only part [of her clothing that could be seen] was a pair of handsomely worked buckskin leggings. Arctic rubbers covered her feet...

Indian Bureau employee Henry Andrews took the Ute delegation to their hotel. Andrews and a city police officer moved into the hotel to supervise the Utes' visit. The Utes ate their meals in a private dining room and did not go out of the hotel without a guard.

Secretary Schurz welcomed Chipeta as a member of the delegation. The first meeting on Tuesday morn-ing was short. The three White River Utes present were not the ones accused of the Meeker crimes. Schurz sent Charles Adams back to Colorado to round up the accused.

The rest of the delegation waited thirty-five days in Washington. Much of the time Chipeta and the other

During the 35 days that the Ute delegation waited in the Tremont House hotel in Washington, an artist drew this illustration for the Frank Leslie's Illustrated Newspaper. It was published in April 1880. Chipeta is on the left.

Utes were confined to the hotel. Henry Andrews allowed a reporter to visit the delegation. The article in *Frank Leslie's Illustrated Newspaper* described Chipeta:

> ...her laugh has a quality of sweetness so rare among her white sisters...She is a stout and comely squaw, gorgeous in a red plaid gown and beaded leggings, her fingers loaded with rings, and her wrists with bracelets, a fashion-

able white canvas bag hanging from one side of her belt, and a beaded pouch from the other, which last she slaps with a burst of merry childish laughter when Major Andrews points it out as her money purse.

Agent Berry took the Ute men shopping for "civilized" clothing. Each man received one suit, two pair of underwear, and two shirts. Berry bought them fashionable stiff collars, ties, and handkerchiefs. Shoes, socks, and hats completed the outfits.

Henry Andrews accompanied Chipeta to Trunnel, Clark & Company. She selected fabrics, and the store recommended a seamstress to make Chipeta's new clothes. Mrs. Rountree spent six days sewing a stylish dress from eight yards of fabric. Chipeta's wardrobe included four dresses plus undergarments. The bill for Mrs. Rountree's work totaled $27.00. The Indian Bureau paid for all the new clothing.

Henry Andrews took the Utes on sight-seeing trips. They toured army and navy bases. They visited George Washington's home, Mount Vernon. On an overnight trip, they saw the new Carlisle Indian School in Pennsylvania.

Delegation Expense Records, National Archives and Records Administration, Record Group 75, Box 1880, #629

While she was in Washington, D.C., Chipeta shopped for fabric for new clothes. Among her purchases on May 27, 1880, Mrs. Ouray (Chipeta) bought yards of flannel, cotton, silk, and thread, needles, and buttons. The receipt for her purchases is now part of our National Archives.

Chipeta and Ouray were invited to social events. They saw a variety show at Ford's Opera House and attended a dinner and dance hosted by the Knights of Columbus. Several times the couple had dinner with Secretary Schurz at his home. The Secretary himself taught Chipeta to play a few simple tunes on his piano.

Chipeta and Ouray posed for photographer Matthew Brady on January 29, 1880. The image above and on the facing page are from a single wet plate negative.

Brady made additional photographs of the couple as well as individual portraits. While Brady's other photographs have been reproduced, these were not printed due to the crack in the glass plate visible in these pictures.

Know More!

Mathew Brady, Photographer

Mathew Brady became famous in the 1860s for photographs of Civil War camps and battlefields. He used a new method called "wet plate negatives." These pictures on glass plates could be printed on paper many times. Earlier photo methods made one image on a metal plate that could not be copied. Brady's studio was busy. His customers included presidents of the United States, government officials, and visitors to the nation's capitol. Collecting pictures of family, friends, and famous people was a popular hobby in the late 1800s.

On January 29, 1880, Chipeta and Ouray posed for the famous photographer Mathew Brady. His studio above Gilman's Drug Store on Pennsylvania Avenue was a popular stop for visitors to the city.

Letters from the clerk at Los Pinos brought welcome contact with home. General Adams wrote to Ouray that the reservation was calm. The letter ended, "tell Chipeta to enjoy herself, not worry and not be sick. Your friend, C. Adams."

The stay in Washington was quiet until Colorado Governor Pitkin arrived. He talked to every newspaper reporter he could find. Describing the Utes as "uncivilized, savage, roaming nomads," Pitkin made threats. If the government did not remove the Utes, the people of Colorado would kill the Indians.

Pitkin also identified the key issue in the conflict. He said the Utes stood in the way of "opening the best lands in the state...the mineral wealth of the unsettled part is exceedingly great." Citizens of the new state wanted the 12,000,000 acre Ute reservation land for the gold and other minerals.

The *Washington Post* supported the Utes. Some people want to "hold a whole tribe responsible for the crimes of a few of its members," the *Post* said. That "would be as reasonable...[as] to call for the hanging of all citizens of Washington" for crimes committed by a few people. The *Post* placed part of the blame on the U.S. government for failure to deliver the Utes' annuities.

At last, the missing White River Utes arrived in the capital. They told their stories to Indian Bureau officials. Secretary Schurz decided the whole White River band must be punished for the deaths at Meeker. They must leave Colorado. Schurz assigned them to a reservation in Utah where the Uintah band of Utes had lived for many years.

That was not the only change Schurz made. He moved the Southern Utes to the very southwest corner of Colorado. He offered the Tabeguache Utes a smaller reservation where the Gunnison River and the Grand River, now named the Colorado River, met.

The Utes did not argue. On March 6, 1880, they accepted Schurz's plan. The delegation needed to convince three-fourths of all Ute males in Colorado to sign the agreement by October 15, 1880.

Official photograph of delegates to the 1880 Ute Treaty Council in Washington. This is one of four photographs often pasted together to show the entire group. From left to right: Ignacio, Carl Shurz (Secretary of the Interior), Woretsiz (standing), Ouray, General Charles Adams (standing), Chipeta.

Colorado Historical Society, #1003892S.

Before returning home, Chipeta, Ouray and several White River Utes testified before a congressional inquiry panel. Chipeta answered the questions of a group of white men on March 19, 1880. She spoke in Ute through an interpreter. She had not witnessed the events at White River, and most of her replies were, "I know nothing."

7 Life Alone

Ouray was worn out when they returned to the farm. Chipeta worried about his condition. His kidney disease was worse. A doctor had been called several times to the hotel in Washington.

The Southern Utes met in August to discuss signing the treaty. Ouray gathered all his energy to attend. He refused to travel in the carriage he had used for several years and rode his horse on the 150-mile trip. McCook, and his wife, Haseekep, rode along with Chipeta and Ouray. They reached the council site near Ignacio, Colorado, on August 18. Two men had to help Ouray off his horse. Chipeta put him to bed in the teepee. She called for a Ute medicine man and the agency doctor.

There was no medicine to save Ouray. He died on August 24, 1880.

Chipeta and Haseekep washed his body. Chipeta painted her husband with sacred colors to protect his spirit as he traveled to join the ancestors. McCook rolled Ouray's body in a buffalo robe and tied it on the back of a horse. McCook, Buckskin Charlie, and two other men led the way into the hills. Chipeta sang ancient songs to soothe Ouray's spirit as she followed the men. They laid the body in a natural gap between some large boulders and packed rocks around it. McCook killed three of Ouray's horses and left them beside the burial place.

Chipeta chopped off her hair and painted her face with charcoal and pine pitch as a sign of mourning. The men burned the teepee where Ouray died and everything inside.

When she returned to the farm, Chipeta gave away all of Ouray's things. She wrapped the fringed and

Know More!

Ouray's Shirt

Ouray's shirt, which Chipeta sent to Carl Schurz, was returned to Colorado in 1977. It can be seen at the Ute Indian Museum at Montrose, Colorado. The medicine bundles Chipeta sewed to the shoulders of the shirt before they left for Washington are still attached.

beaded shirt he so recently wore to Washington and sent it along with Ouray's beaded tobacco pouch and powder horn to Carl Schurz.

In his memoirs, Schurz recalled the gift and Chipeta's letter to him:

> [Chipeta said] I had done much to save Ouray's people from disaster...If I accepted the present... it would be regarded by Chipeta and her people as proof of true friendship on my part, and they would esteem that friendship very highly. But if I made a present in return it would be understood by them as signifying that I did not value their friendship much and simply wished to get rid of an obligation and be quits with them.

Ouray's death halted discussion of the new treaty. Settlers feared the Utes might start a war without Ouray to control them.

When the Southern Utes met again, the men did not want to sign the treaty. Otto Mears paid two dollars to each man who would pick up the pen and put his mark on the paper. The agreement was completed.

Many routines changed for Chipeta. Ouray's government salary stopped at his death. Chipeta had no income to buy supplies. Now, she lined up with the other Ute women for rations of flour, sugar, and coffee.

Chipeta's brother, Sapovanara, became head chief of the Tabeguache. Chiefs and headmen still came to the farm to consult Chipeta on important matters. In May 1881, Chipeta visited the military men guarding the reservation. She reported some White River Utes were trying to gather guns and warriors for one last war against the white men. She spoke for her people. The Tabeguache want no trouble, she said.

President Hayes named a team of men, including Otto Mears, to oversee the Tabeguache move to the new reservation land. Mears said the land on the Grand River was not good for farming. He convinced the team to settle the Utes in Utah instead. The treaty allowed this change, but no one had explained that to the chiefs when they signed the treaty. The chiefs refused to move to Utah.

Agent Berry insisted the Utes with farms be paid for improvements made to their land. Chipeta's farm, Berry said, was the most valuable. Her property was described in an August 11, 1881 report:

Improved farm on Uncompahgre River consisting of fenced cultivated fields, irrigation ditches, hay meadow, story and half residence containing four rooms, four tenement houses, mess house [separate kitchen building], carriage house, tool house, horse barn, chicken house and three vegetable cellars. Appraised value $5,000.

On August 27, 1881, Chipeta loaded her pack horse and a wagon. Some boys drove the livestock. They joined 1,458 Utes forced to leave the Uncompahgre Valley under supervision of the army. Each family received three weeks rations of beef, flour, hard bread, and salt for the trip. Agent Berry brought 600 pounds of sugar, 250 pounds of coffee, and 50 pounds of tobacco the government had refused to deliver.

The procession followed the Gunnison River, right through the land where the Utes had expected to live. They crossed the Grand River on flatboats and rode into Utah. Both Agent Berry and Otto Mears traveled with the Utes. Berry was a welcome friend who continued to serve as Ute agent in Utah. Mears was a traitor in the eyes of the Utes. At least one Ute attempted to kill Mears during the trip.

8 Utah Reservation

The government named the new reservation "Ouray." In contrast to the beautiful Uncompahgre Valley, this land was brown and bare. The government promised Chipeta a house in Utah like the one Ouray built. She received an unfinished two room cabin. Chipeta soon abandoned the house and lived in her teepee. She set up camp with her brother McCook and his family. In summer, they grazed sheep in western Colorado high country where the grass was good. In the winter, they returned to Utah and camped in a valley along Bitter Creek.

A young man named Newton Castle arrived in western Colorado in 1883. He began trade with the Utes. One winter he met Chipeta. He recalled they talked in a combination of English, Spanish, and sign language.

She wanted to know about the Uncompahgre Valley, how it had changed since she left. Castle described ranches and growing towns. Chipeta ended their meeting shaking her head and saying, "Too much fences."

Despite the difficulties of life in Utah, Chipeta was happy with her family. Within four years she found a second husband and adopted a teepee full of boys. On June 30, 1885, Agent J. F. Gardner recorded the names, ages, and family relationships of all Utes at the Ouray Agency. The agent wrote Ute names in syllables to show how they were pronounced. Household #122 included:

Ac cum moo quats	Husband	Male	47
Chi pi ta	Wife	Female	43
Dou as cu no	Ward	Male	15
Se vi to	Ward	Male	13
Guadaloupe	Ward	Male	9
Jose La Cross	Ward	Male	7
John Peto	Ward	Male	4
Francisco	Ward	Male	5

McCook, age 36, was recorded in the census with his 24-year-old wife, Hah see kep, and 2-year-old son, Sea goots. Sap po va na ra, age 53, and his wife,

Keo ra ra pan, age 48, had three wards living with them. McCook and Sapovanara approved the census information along with fifteen other chiefs and head men. Accummooquats was neither a chief nor a head man.

The Ute agent listed Accummooquats, McCook, and Sapovanara among forty-eight of the best men on the reservation. The agent said these men showed good sense and energy. They worked hard and promoted good understanding between the Indians and the government.

In the summer of 1887, Chipeta and Accummooquats grazed their sheep on western Colorado land. McCook and several other Ute families were with them. In August, the men and older boys of the camp went hunting. McCook left to take care of business on the reservation. Chipeta and five women, with eight children, managed the main camp and looked after the sheep.

One day the Garfield County sheriff rode into camp with a posse of 150 cowboys. They were looking for some Utes who stole horses from a local rancher. The rowdy cowboys pointed at the Ute women and made rude comments. Chipeta told the sheriff the Utes in her camp wanted no trouble. She said they did not steal horses. Chipeta told the sheriff and his men to leave.

Chipeta feared the cowboys might come back. She gathered the women and children and hid behind some boulders on the mountain side. From this hiding place they watched the cowboys return, loot the camp, and set fire to two teepees. Chipeta knew better than to risk staying in the camp. She did not know where to find Accummooquats and the other men. A Ute called Old Colorow had a camp to the north. Leaving the sheep and goats grazing on the mountainside, Chipeta led the women and children north.

They had not walked far when Chipeta heard the cowboys coming behind them. Two of the Ute boys fired their rifles at the men. Chipeta heard the sheriff yell at the cowboys. He said they were searching for horse thieves, not a bunch of women and children. The cowboys rode away.

Chipeta was relieved when she found Old Colorow's camp. Her little group welcomed food and water after the long walk. Old Colorow's men rode to a store near the town of Meeker for supplies. The storekeeper returned with the men. There was big trouble, the storekeeper warned. Stories about theft of a few horses had grown into rumors that the Utes were burning and looting homes. The frightened citizens asked the governor for help. Three hundred fifty **militia** men plus armed citizens guarded the town of Meeker. The governor ordered all Utes back to the reservation. Local citizens threatened to shoot them on sight.

Chipeta and the women helped pack the camp. They began moving westward at sunrise with Old Colorow's sheep and cattle.

Chipeta and Old Colorow's group drove the livestock through heavy rains. On August 24, they camped for the night along a river at the edge of the reservation. Chipeta was cooking breakfast the next morning when militia men started shooting. A Ute named Atchee ran up the hill and shouted in English, "Stop shooting. There are women and children in camp." A militia man shot him in the leg. The Ute men moved downriver and the women and children escaped in the opposite direction.

Chipeta arrived at the agency on August 27. Accummooquats and his hunting party appeared a short time later. When everyone had returned, the agent counted one Ute man and three children killed. Others were wounded.

(Gunnison Rebiew

October 9, 1887

In Time of Peace Prepare for War

The Citizens of Gunnison Organizing for a Ute Outbreak

"Trust in God and Keep Your Powder Dry."

WAR!

In view of the present condition of the Utes it is deemed advisable to organize for protection.

Chipeta did not know she was national news. The *New York Times* reported the events in Colorado. The paper noted "grave fears" for Chipeta's safety after her camp was attacked and burned.

In September, a U.S. Indian Inspector investigated the attack. He reported the cowboys took 600 horses, 37 cows, and 2,300 sheep and goats that belonged to the Utes. The Inspector said Chipeta purchased her sheep and goats with money left by her husband,

Chief Ouray. All of her property was stolen or destroyed. Colorado officials returned 450 sheep and goats to the reservation in November.

A year later, Special Agent H. S. Welton visited the reservation. Chipeta was among the thirty chiefs and headmen who met with him on October 1, 1888. Chipeta and Old Colorow asked to go to Washington. The head chief of the United States would repay their $32,000 loss of livestock, they said. Although Welton recommended the Indian Bureau allow Chipeta, Sapovanara, and Old Colorow to travel to Washington, they did not go. The Ouray agent did not report any money received for the stolen animals.

Know More!

The 1880 Ute Treaty

The 1880 Ute Treaty was unusual. For the first time the government gave land titles to individual Indians rather to the Utes as a group. In his December 6, 1880, annual message to congress, President Rutherford B. Hayes wrote, "...for the first time in history of the country an Indian nation has given up its tribal existence to be settled in **severalty** and to live as individuals under the common protection of the laws of the country." In the past, Indians owned their reservations "in common" or as a group.

Sapovanara died of a liver ailment in January 1889. A **diphtheria** epidemic struck the reservation in 1890 and probably claimed Accummooquats. Chipeta was listed as head of household with the six boys in the 1891 reservation census. By 1894 only the three youngest boys remained with Chipeta. An 18-year-old female ward named Laupeta had joined the family.

In the late 1890s the government decided to complete a provision of the 1880 treaty. Each adult Ute received title to a piece of land, called an *allotment*. After all allotments were made, the government could sell unclaimed land to outsiders.

On February 1, 1898, the agent for the Ouray Reservation reported 232 allotments completed. Chipeta claimed 160 acres on White River. McCook had 160 acres on Bitter Creek where he and Chipeta and their family spent part of every year. Chipeta's youngest ward (John Peto) recorded his allotment under the name J. P. Chipeta.

Agents assigned to the Utes reported that Chipeta and McCook were among the most influential members of the Tabeguache band. Chipeta was not a chief, but chiefs and headmen still consulted her and valued her opinions. One of the few documented cases of her participation in a council of chiefs took place in December 1910.

A new agent, Captain Brees, held a council with the Tabeguache chiefs to hear their concerns. Brees asked his clerk to make a written record of what each chief said. McCook spoke first. He complained outsiders were grazing sheep on Ute land. A few chiefs asked for an irrigation ditch to increase farmland.

Chipeta was the fifth speaker and the only woman. She told Agent Brees the government failed to keep its promise to give her "a good house to live in and a good living" in Utah. She supported McCook's complaint about sheep. "These sheep men tell their herders that this land does not belong to the Indians," Chipeta said.

Agent Brees suggested the Utes brand their livestock so the animals could be identified, if stolen by the outsiders. Chipeta set an example. Her sheep soon displayed the Flying Ute brand, a wide "U" shape with wings on the tips and a "T" in the middle.

9 Honored Guest

By the turn of the new century, feelings against the Utes had eased. Chipeta's old friend, Margaret Adams, began a campaign to help Chipeta in her old age. In a 1903 article for the *Colorado Springs Gazette*, Mrs. Adams wrote, "Chipeta...is now alone, poor and forgotten, on a barren reservation in Utah, where even an experienced farmer could not make a living, much less an old Indian woman." Mrs. Adams did more than ask for donations. She begged the women of Colorado to write letters to Colorado senators and representatives asking for a special fund to support Chipeta. The special fund failed, but Chipeta benefited from being in the news.

Old friends and strangers welcomed Chipeta back to Colorado. Stories of her past efforts to maintain peace were told everywhere she went. Communities invited her to special events. Her hosts took her for rides in automobiles to show "improvements" made in the Ute homeland. Chipeta smiled politely and said she was impressed.

In 1909, workmen completed drilling a 5.8 mile tunnel through the mountains to irrigate the Uncompahgre Valley. The water came from the Gunnison River. Chipeta was a special guest at the ceremony opening the Gunnison Tunnel. She stopped first in Grand Junction the morning of September 23, 1909, to hear a speech by President William Howard Taft. Chipeta was invited to meet the president. He was a very large man and had to bend over to hear Chipeta's words.

Taft learned that Chipeta was going on to Montrose for the tunnel dedication. He insisted she ride to the railroad station in his car. Late that same afternoon, Chipeta stood beside a deep ravine on the edge of the Uncompahgre Valley. At a signal from President Taft, workmen miles away released the water. It roared through the long tunnel to irrigate farmland in the valley Chipeta loved.

In the summer of 1911, Chipeta was invited to the Montrose Fourth of July celebration where she

Life was harder for Chipeta on the dry and barren Ouray Reservation in Utah. She was photographed on the reservation in 1907.

received a gift of silver coins. She received another gift of money in the town of Ouray.

Chipeta arrived on the Southern Ute Reservation in late July. Chief Buckskin Charlie had an invitation to visit Colorado Springs. The town wanted a group of Utes to be a special attraction for the town's fortieth anniversary. Chipeta was eager to go. By the end of the month, she slept in a familiar spot in South Cheyenne Canyon. She had camped there often with Ouray to hunt buffalo. Chipeta rode in a parade of Colorado Springs pioneers and joined in demonstrating traditional Ute dances.

Chipeta and the Southern Utes returned to Colorado Springs a month later to participate in a new town festival called Shan Kive. Townspeople arranged a special reunion for Chipeta and Margaret Adams. The two old friends rode together in the back seat of a touring car in the Shan Kive parade. They spent the afternoon recalling their days at Los Pinos agency on Cochetopa Pass.

Chipeta was pleased that people in Colorado remembered her. She was honored with gifts wherever she went. The United States government, Chipeta thought, seemed to have forgotten her.

In March 1916, former Indian agent Jewell Martin wrote a letter to the Commissioner of Indian Affairs. Martin described Chipeta as "destitute." He asked the government to provide some "creature comforts" for Chipeta in her old age. Commissioner Cato Sells asked Albert Kneale at the Utah agency for a report.

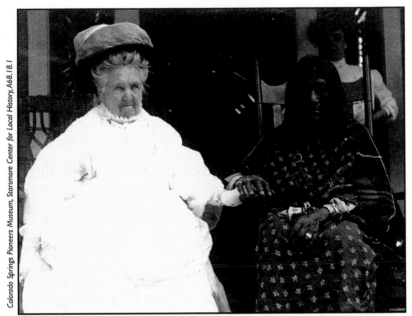

Old friends Margaret Adams and Chipeta held hands on the front porch of # 6 Boulder Crescent, Colorado Springs, after the Shan Kive parade in August 1911.

Kneale spent several days in Chipeta's camp. He found Chipeta and McCook to be "careful and thoughtful people."

Kneale sent Sells an eight-page letter. The government had not kept its promises to Chipeta or the Utes, Kneale said. Irrigation water never came to make farmland of the barren Utah reservation. Kneale recommended that irrigating the land was the best thing Sells could do for Chipeta.

Sells had no interest in an expensive irrigation project. He offered to buy Chipeta some furniture for her house. Chipeta had no use for furniture in her teepee, Kneale replied. He described Chipeta as an Indian of the old school who wore a blanket, painted her face with **vermillion**, and ate and slept on the ground. Kneale suggested Chipeta would appreciate something simple, a blanket or shawl. Cato Sells sent Chipeta a shawl and a letter on October 16, 1916.

Chipeta sent Commissioner Sells a photo of herself wearing the shawl. She also sent him a saddle blanket. The Indian agent wrote Chipeta's words in a letter to Sells. She ended her letter saying, "I am also glad that there is no more trouble existing between the Indians and the white people, and hope that this state of affairs exists through the rest of my life time." Chipeta signed the typewritten letter with her thumb print, and the Ute agent wrote her name below.

Physical ailments increased as Chipeta aged. She and McCook often traveled to mineral hot springs in Colorado to soak her aching joints. One favorite spring became a health spa and tourist attraction in the town of Glenwood Springs. Elmer Lewis, manager of the Hotel Colorado, invited Chipeta and McCook to visit

Chipeta sent this photograph made in October 1916 to Cato Sells, Commissioner of Indian Affairs. The shawl she is wearing was a gift from Commissioner Sells.

Denver Public Library, Western History Collection, Z-1373.

as his guests. Chipeta told other guests about times when she and Ouray soaked in the springs before the white man came. "Boiling water make me well then, make me well now again," she said.

A government assessment of health issues on the reservation found an **epidemic** of trachoma in 1914. This infection caused the upper eyelid to swell and turn inward so the eyelashes scratched the **cornea**. It was a painful illness that often caused blindness. Edith Richardson, a nurse at a small hospital near the reservation, assisted Dr. Lloyd in treating Chipeta for trachoma. She described Chipeta as "warm, friendly and cultured" even while suffering such a painful disease.

Trachoma was not easily cured and reinfection was common. Mrs. W. G. King, a nurse who worked near Dragon, Utah, also treated Chipeta for trachoma.

> One day Chipeta came in to see me about her eyes. I telephoned to her doctor and he gave me instructions for treatments. Hot packs were to be put on her eyes, and he sent medicine to be dropped into them. I explained she must have treatment for a long period of time in order to get relief and to have improved eyesight. The Indians were very cooperative. They moved down from their camp on bitter creek and made camp…a short way from Dragon.

Chipeta's eye problems continued. She developed **cataracts** that limited her sight. McCook tied ropes from the teepee to the trees so she would not get lost while doing chores. Chipeta's niece laid out bowls, each holding beads of one color, in the order Chipeta requested. Chipeta decorated bags, moccasins, and **cradleboards** by memory and feel.

In September 1921, McCook took Chipeta to St. Mary's Hospital in Grand Junction for eye surgery. A new friend, William Weiser, paid her expenses. Dr. Guy Cary donated his services.

Chipeta spent seven weeks in the little brick hospital on Colorado Avenue. She asked to have her bed placed on a second floor porch instead of in a room. She wanted to smell the air, feel the sunshine, and hear the chickens, cows, and goats the hospital kept in the backyard.

After the surgery, nurses packed bags of sand around Chipeta's head. They told her to lie flat on her back and not move while her eyes healed. Chipeta would not stay in bed. The surgery failed. Chipeta returned home with limited vision in one eye. She could see only light and shadow in the other eye.

10 Return to Colorado

Limited eyesight in her final years did not keep Chipeta from traveling. With McCook as her guide, she made her annual trips to Colorado. A **narrow gauge** railroad line from Dragon, Utah, to Mack, Colorado, opened in 1905. When riding long distances on a horse became difficult, Chipeta rode the train. Mr. Banks, manager of the Uintah Railroad office at Dragon, remembered Chipeta's hands. "[They were] very large all over and they showed the abuse of hard work...She was very kind and considerate. She made a pair of moccasins for me and a purse for my wife."

Chipeta died in her teepee on Bitter Creek on August 16, 1924. McCook carried her blanket wrapped body into the hills and buried her in an unmarked grave.

A week later, the Indian agent at the Southern Ute Reservation in Colorado arranged for Ouray's bones to be removed from their burial place. The agent hoped to bring Chipeta's body back to Colorado to be reburied with Ouray's remains. He contacted the Indian agent at the Ouray Reservation about the plan. He also requested government funds to build a monument on the planned gravesite.

The Daughters of the American Revolution (DAR) in Montrose, Colorado, also offered a plan. They proposed reburying Chipeta near the farm she and Ouray loved. The DAR had recently built a memorial to Chipeta and Ouray. It was a concrete teepee that sheltered the spring where Chipeta had collected fresh water.

The agent in Utah consulted McCook. The requests were unusual, but McCook understood. The people in Colorado remembered Chipeta and wanted to honor her. He chose the old farm. McCook left the decision about reburial of Ouray to the Southern Utes.

Chipeta made her final trip to Colorado by train, accompanied as always by McCook. Five thousand people gathered on Sunday, March 15, 1925, to witness Chipeta's burial. A mile-long procession of people and automobiles followed the plain wooden coffin across snow-packed ground. McCook led the solemn parade to the burial site. The Montrose Band marched behind him, followed by units of the Colorado National Guard, Boy Scouts, Grand Army of the Republic, Women's Relief Corps, Daughters of Veterans, and the DAR.

McCook and a small group gathered inside the DAR's memorial teepee for a drink of water from the spring. Reverend Hersey, from the Episcopal church near the Utah reservation, offered a blessing for Chipeta. "May the memory of your heroic and humanitarian deeds be kept fragrant in the hearts and thoughts of the white people, whom you so faithfully served."

McCook said, "Chipeta, I have brought you home."

The funeral service began at 3:00 p.m. The band played "America." An official of the Ouray Agency presented Chipeta's remains to the people of Colorado. McCook laid a piece of Chipeta's beaded buckskin on the coffin and spoke a farewell in Ute. Reverend Hersey led the Episcopal funeral service. DAR ladies placed a wreath and a flag beside the tomb. With hands over their hearts, the assembled guests sang "The Star Spangled Banner." A bugler played "Taps" to end the service.

Chipeta's brother, McCook, stands beside the memorial teepee near Chipeta's tomb. The teepee is on the site of the farm where she lived in the Uncompahgre Valley, 1925.

The DAR attempted to place Ouray's remains beside Chipeta. McCook told the Southern Ute chiefs he would like to see the couple buried together, but the chiefs declined.

On May 24, 1925, the Southern Utes held their own elaborate ceremony. They buried the bones reported to be the remains of Ouray in the cemetery at Ignacio.

Chipeta's faithful brother, McCook, was buried beside her in 1937.

Chipeta was not forgotten. The people of Colorado named many places in her honor. In 1976, Colorado celebrated 100 years as a state. A **centennial tapestry** was created to honor women in Colorado history. A committee chose eighteen women who played important roles in the settlement and development of the state. Chipeta was honored for her efforts as a peacemaker. The art work, called the "Women's Gold Tapestry," hangs in the state capitol building.

Know More!

Queen of the Utes

The first time Chipeta was called "Queen of the Utes," the title was meant as an insult. A reporter went to Los Pinos with Governor McCook for the 1872 treaty council. The reporter found nothing good to say about the Utes. He called them **hyenas** and **vermin**. He made fun of their clothing and their behavior. His article appeared in the *Rocky Mountain News*, September 11, 1872. About Chipeta, he wrote:

> This afternoon the commissioners were visited upon by the queen of the Utes — Madame Ure I suppose she is called — who swept down in all her royal stations, attired in a skirt of buckskin, a pair of moccasins, an old shawl, and a lot of uncombed hair.

Poet Eugene Field used the term "Queen of the Utes" in a positive way in an 1882 poem. However, Field turned Chipeta into the heroine of the hostage taking at White River. Some people still believe Chipeta jumped on her horse, rode alone through the night, and rescued the captive Meeker women and children.

When Chipeta died in 1924, the *Denver Post* headline read, "Queen Chipeta Rejoins Husband, Chief Ouray, In Happy Hunting Ground." This time, the title of "Queen" honored a beloved woman.

About Chipeta

"She was a brave woman, of course. She accepted the situation that her husband, and his influence, would bring on her. She was loyal to her husband, stood by him all the time, even when his purposes were futile...I think she filled her role adequately."

— Roland McCook, Chipeta's great nephew, from an interview with Susan Lyman-Whitney for the book Worth Their Salt

"Everyone on the reservation called Chipeta their grandmother."

— J. Monaghan, interviews with Utes on the reservation by CWA workers, 1933-34, Colorado Historical Society

"When I first knew Chipeta she was the brightest and handsomest squaw in the tribe...she was always laughing, always singing, ever doing kind acts toward the poorest of her people, and was greatly loved by them."

— Margaret T. Adams (Mrs. Charles Adams)

"The Government will take care of Chi-pe-ta as long as she lives. Ouray's widow shall never come to want."

— Agent Berry to Ute chiefs, quoted by A. B. Meacham in a letter to the Secretary of the Interior, August 26, 1880

"[Chipeta was] an intelligent, lovable person, and I never once heard her complain. She was the kindest person I ever knew."

— *Laura Foster, cook at the gilsonite mine near Dragon, Utah*

"Chipeta was good hearted, always offering you something. McCook same way. A good honest feller...They played cards a lot — [games called] 'coon can' and 'monte'."

— *Claude Taylor, Chipeta's Bitter Creek neighbor for 41 years*

Timeline

1843 – Chipeta is born

1848 – U.S. settles war with Mexico. Southwest becomes U.S. territory.

1859 – Chipeta marries Ouray. Gold is discovered in Colorado.

1861 – Colorado Territory is organized.

1863 – Ouray makes first of six trips to Washington, D.C. Ouray's son, Pahlone, is stolen by Plains Indians.

1868 – 14th Amendment to U.S. Constitution gives citizenship to all persons born in the U.S., except Native Americans.

1869 – Chipeta and Ouray get first house at Los Pinos Agency on Cochetopa Pass.

1872 – Felix Brunot offers to bring Pahlone home, if Ouray gives up San Juan Mountain lands.

1873 – Ouray goes to Washington, D.C. to meet the Arapaho boy who may be Pahlone.

1874 – Chipeta and Ouray build a house and start farming in Uncompahgre Valley.

1876 – Colorado becomes a state.

1879 – Northern Utes kill soldiers, their Indian agent, and workers at White River Agency, and take women and children hostage.

1880 – Chipeta and Ouray lead Ute delegation to Washington. Chipeta testifies before Congressional inquiry panel. Ouray dies in Colorado.

1881 – Chipeta and the Utes are forced to relocate to Utah reservation. Chipeta marries second husband and adopts six boys.

1887 – Chipeta and other Utes attacked while herding sheep in Colorado.

1893 – Colorado becomes first state in which men voted to grant voting rights to women. Indian women not included.

1909 – Chipeta attends opening of Gunnison Tunnel with President William Howard Taft.

1911 & 1913 – Chipeta attends Shan Kive in Colorado Springs.

1920 – Nineteenth Amendment to U.S. Constitution gives women right to vote, but excludes Indian women.

1924 – Indians become U.S. citizens. Chipeta dies and is buried in Utah.

1925 – Chipeta's remains are reburied near Montrose, Colorado. Ouray is reburied in Ignacio, Colorado.

New Words

adobe – sun-dried bricks made of mud and straw

agent – a person acting on behalf of another person, group or organization

annuities – annual payments

awl – a pointed tool for making holes in leather

cataract – cloudiness in the lens of the eye

centennial – one-hundred-year anniversary

Cochetopa – from a Ute word meaning "pass of the buffalo"

Commissioner – an official in charge of a department of government or public service

Conejos – Spanish for "rabbits"

Continental Divide – the highest mountains on the North American continent; rivers flow east or west from this mountain range.

cornea – the transparent covering over the iris and pupil of the eye

cradleboards – baby carriers that strap on the mother's back

delegation – a group of persons chosen to represent others

diphtheria – a disease that makes breathing difficult. It is easily passed from one person to another

epidemic – an outbreak of disease that affects many people at one time

hostages – people held captive to insure demands are met

hyenas – animals that look similar to dogs; found in Asia and Africa

narrow gauge – railroad tracks set close together, often used in mountain areas where passages are narrow. The distance between standard tracks is 4 feet, $8^1/_2$ inches. Typical narrow gauge tracks are 3 feet, 6 inches apart.

Los Pinos – Spanish for "the pines"

militia – army units called on in emergencies

piñon – a kind of pine that produces edible seeds

reservation – land set aside for a special use

Secretary of the Interior – government official responsible for the nation's land and natural resources

severalty – right to own property that is not shared with any other person

Tabeguache – a Ute word meaning "people who live on the warm side of the mountain"

tanned – turning animal hide (skin) into leather. The Utes worked the brains of the animal into the hide, soaked the hide in water, and dried it.

tapestry – a wall hanging created by weaving fibers into a picture

territory – an area or region that is home to a group of people

Territory – a part of the United States, not included in any state, with its own elected officials and governing system

Uncompahgre – from a Ute word meaning "red lake"

vermillion – red color. The Utes ground red dirt or rock and mixed it with animal fat to make a paint

vermin – unwanted pests that are hard to get rid of

Sources

"A Colorado Tragedy," *Harper's Weekly*, October 17, 1874, p. 852.

Davis, Georgie A. "Illustrated Interview of our lady artist with the Ute Indian Chiefs and prisoners in Washington, D.C.," *Frank Leslie's Illustrated Journal*, April 1880.

Dawson, Thomas F., "Interview with James B. Thompson," *The Trail*, August 1924, Vol XVI #3, pgs 6-13.

Denver Post, Aug. 25, 1924.

Denver Times, May 21, 1902.

Dunlay, Tom. *Kit Carson & the Indians*, Lincoln: University of Nebraska Press, 2000.

Durango Democrat, July 12, 1911.

Colorado Springs Gazette, Oct. 11, 1903.

Grand Junction Sentinel, March 15, 1925.

Gunnison Review, July 10, 1880; October 9, 1880; April 2, 1881.

Hafen, LeRoy R. and Ann W., Editors. *The Diaries of William Henry Jackson Frontier Photographer*, Glendale, Calif: The Arthur H. Clark Company, 1959.

Jocknick, Sidney. *Early Days on the Western Slope*, Montrose, Colo: Western Reflections Publishing, 1913, 1988.

Journal of the Western Slope, Vol 1 No 2, 1986 and Vol 8 No 2, 1993.

King, Mrs. W.G. "Our Ute Indians," *Colorado Magazine*, Vol XXXVII #2, April 1960, pgs 128-132.

Lyman-Whitney, Susan. "Chipeta: She Didn't Want to Come to Utah," *Worth Their Salt*, Boulder, Colo: NetLibrary, Inc., 1999.

McClellan, Val J. *This Is Our Land, Vol II*, Jamestown, Ohio: Western Publishers, 1979.

McNitt, Frank. *The Indian Traders*, Norman: University of Oklahoma Press, 1962.

Meeker, Josephine. *The Ute Massacre*, Vic Press, 1974 (reprint of 1879 original).

Ouray Plaindealer, July 7, 1911.

Ouray Times, Oct. 25, 1879.

Pettit, Jan. *Utes: the Mountain People*, Boulder, Colo: Johnson Books, 1990.

Santala, Major Russel D. *The Ute Campaign of 1879: A Study in the Use of the Military Instrument*, U.S. Government Printing Office, 1994.

Shaputis, June and Suzanne Kelly. *A History of Chaffee County*, Buena Vista Heritage, 1982.

"Testimony in Relation to Ute Outbreak," 46th Congress, 2nd Session, House Miscellaneous Documents No. 38, 1880, pg 191.

The Vernal Express (Utah), May 26, 1932; Dec. 11, 1941.

Viola, Herman. *Diplomats in Buckskin*, Blufton, S. Car: Rivilo Books, 1995.

Washington Evening Star, October 24, 1873.

Washington Post, January 12, 20, 23, 27, 30, 1880; March 4, 1880.

OTHER SOURCES

Dawson Collection, Colorado Historical Society, Denver, CO.

Doris Duke Collection (interviews) and Manuscript Collection Boxes 7, 10 and 12, Marriott Library, University of Utah, Salt Lake City, UT.

Goss, James, Professor, Texas Tech University, workshop on Ute history and culture, Western State College, Alamosa, Colorado, 1995

MWG Dean Collection, Museum of Western History, Grand Junction, CO.

National Archives, Bureau of Indian Affairs Correspondence, U.S. Government Documents 0246, NARA Record Group 11, M448 and Delegation Expense Records; NARA Record Group 75, Box 2337-C-1863; Box 1880; Special Case 112; U.S. Indian Census Rolls, 1884-1940. NARA Record Group 75, M234, Roll 204

Tour of old St. Mary's Hospital and review of original hospital register with Dave Fishell, Grand Junction, CO, December 13, 2001.

WEB SITES

Chipeta Elementary School web site, Colorado Springs, Colorado http://www.cssd11.k12.co.us/chipeta/WhowasChipeta.htm

Hayden survey maps. http://swcenter.fortlewis.edu/inventory/HaydenMaps.htm

William Henry Jackson photography. http://www.lib.byu.edu/dlib/jackson/

Ute history. http://www.southern-ute.nsn.us

Index

Acknowledgments

Without the encouragement and support of my husband, David Becker, I would not have completed the research and writing for this book. He and the 24Wed critique group offered valuable constructive criticism. My research was aided by the skills and dedication of staff members at the National Archives, National Anthropological Archives, Colorado State Archives, Colorado Historical Society, Denver Public Library Western History Collection, Penrose Public Library Special Collections (Colorado Springs), Starsmore Center for Local History at the Colorado Springs Pioneers Museum, Museum of Western History (Grand Junction), and the University of Utah's Marriott Library Special Collections. My thanks to Dave Fishell of Grand Junction, who took me on a "Chipeta" tour, and Professor Robert Goss, Texas Tech University, who introduced me to Ute history and culture.

About the Author

Cynthia Becker grew up in southern Indiana. A true child of the 1950s, her goal was to be a cowgirl, just like Dale Evans. She loved to read and began writing stories in elementary school. Cynthia moved to Colorado the day after her college graduation and remains a Coloradan.

She began researching the life of Chipeta in 1995. She dug into old Indian Agent reports in the National Archives, searched photographs in the National Anthropological Archives, visited libraries and museums in Colorado and Utah, and read lots of old newspapers. The result was her first book, *Chipeta: Queen of the Utes* (Western Reflections Publishing, 2003). Since then, Cynthia has written five books on current topics for educational publisher Thomson Gale and contributed to an anthology of sports biographies. Her feature articles have appeared in the *New York Times*, the *Saturday Evening Post*, *Colorado Country Life*, *Family Chronicle*, and *Learning Through History*. She was selected a "Colorado Voices" writer by the *Denver Post* in 2003.

For more information on research, writing, and Chipeta visit Cynthia's blog— *www.Chipeta.wordpress.com*.